The Children's
Book of Faith

Edited by
William J. Bennett

Illustrated by
Michael Hague

A Doubleday Book for Young Readers

The Children's
Book of Faith

A Doubleday Book for Young Readers
Published by
Random House Children's Books
a division of Random House, Inc.
1540 Broadway
New York, New York 10036
DOUBLEDAY and the anchor with dolphin colophon are registered
trademarks of Random House, Inc.
Text copyright © 2000 by William J. Bennett
Illustrations copyright © 2000 by Michael Hague
ISBN 0-385-32771-4
The text of this book is set in 13-point Dutch Aster.
Manufactured in the United States of America

Contents

Introduction

Someone once said that at the summit of every noble human endeavor, you find a steeple pointing toward God. You find steeples atop the grand peaks of history—the founding of American democracy, the birth of the modern civil rights movement, the struggle against totalitarianism. You find steeples crowning daily efforts in countless lives—neighbors going out of their way to lend a hand, husbands and wives sharing strength, parents sacrificing their own wants to see to their children's needs.

In a world that often seems full of woe, faith produces an astounding amount of good. It is the rock on which so many virtues are founded: honesty, courage, generosity, hard work, responsibility, and self-control. It is a call to kindness, decency, forgiveness, and love. Faith keeps us from drifting by anchoring our sense of right and wrong. It lifts each person outside himself and offers a larger sense of purpose as we journey through life.

Parents help children learn about faith in several time-tested ways. They pray and read scripture together, as a family. They celebrate holy days. They go to church or temple and take part in activities there. "Go to church!" Teddy Roosevelt advised. "Yes, I know all the excuses. I know that one can worship the Creator and dedicate oneself to good living in a grove of trees or in one's own house. But I also know that as a matter of cold fact the average man does *not* thus worship. If he stays away from church, he does not spend his time in good works or in lofty meditation. He looks over the colored supplement of the newspaper." Above all, parents teach by example.

The stories we share with young children can help too. The selections in this book are meant to inspire young hearts and minds, to help them understand what faith is all about. In these pages, we find examples of people who draw strength from above, trusting in God to help them in the large and small tasks of life. We witness them living in readiness to answer God's call and standing steadfast in their devotion to him. By reading and talking about faith, parents help children learn that God loves them, that he cares about what they do, that he has created them for goodness.

Once again Michael Hague has taken up his brush to set story and verse aglow. His beautiful illustrations cast their illuminating light like stained-glass windows. Michael knows how to lift children's imaginations and call their thoughts toward heaven. His paintings, in their own way, glorify God.

In assembling this book, I have turned to the Judeo-Christian tradition, for some simple reasons. Like most Americans, I am a Christian, and I serve the reader best by sharing what I know and believe. In a very real sense, the Judeo-Christian tradition belongs to all Americans. It is a precious heritage, one that has given birth to our free political institutions and shaped our national ideals. It lies at the foundations of Western civilization. The choice of material is in no way meant to slight or cast doubt on other faiths. This country draws strength from its diversity and firm commitment to religious tolerance. Our freedom to worship as we see fit is, I believe, a great gift of God.

We Americans have received some extraordinary blessings: material comforts, economic prosperity, breathtaking advances in science, medicine, and technology. In the midst of plenty, it is easy to neglect spiritual matters. Our aspirations and desires can turn us toward the wrong things. Our popular culture tends to lure us away from a life of faith, sometimes urging a spiritual torpor. It beckons to children from television and movies, computer screens, radios, stereos, magazines, and even some books. Every thoughtful parent knows it and, on occasion, despairs.

Flannery O'Connor, a writer of deep faith, advised that "you have to push as hard as the age that pushes against you." The good news is that when adults do push against the darker aspects of our time, good things happen for young people. I hope this book aids parents in that task and speaks to children as creatures of God who are beginning a spiritual journey. It aims to help youngsters learn that we all belong to the Almighty, and that we must strive to live in ways that glorify him. I hope that for you and your children, this book will serve as a small steeple pointing toward God.

The Children's Book of Faith

Daniel in the Lions' Den

*Here is one of our greatest examples of someone who
stood firm in his faith.*

Long ago in the land of Babylon, there lived a man
named Daniel. He was a very wise man, so wise, in fact,
that the king of Babylon decided to take him into his service
and put him in charge of much of the kingdom. This made
many of the other noblemen jealous of Daniel. They kept
trying to find a way to turn King Darius against him, but
Daniel was so honest and good that they could find no fault
in him.

Then they had an idea. These men knew that three times
every day, Daniel went to his room, opened the window that
looked toward the city of Jerusalem, which was his home,
and prayed to God.

"We'll use his faith in God to bring him down," they told
each other.

Next they went to King Darius and began to flatter and
praise him.

"You are a great and wise king, Your Majesty," they told
him. "No one is as great as you."

"Yes, you are right," Darius said, nodding.

"You are the one who provides all good things to us," they
said.

"Yes, that's true as well," answered the king.

"We wish to make a new law, so that everyone will know
how great you are," they went on. "For thirty days, no one

shall pray to any god, but only to the king himself. If anyone prays to a god, they shall be thrown to the lions. Now, great king, write the law and sign it, and make it so that it cannot be changed."

The king was a vain man, and he was pleased with the idea of a law that would set him above even the gods. So, without asking Daniel's advice, he signed the new law, and his decree went out through the kingdom. For thirty days, no one would be allowed to worship anyone except the king himself.

Daniel heard that the law had been made, but every day he still went to his room three times, opened the window that looked toward Jerusalem, and offered his prayer to the Lord. Daniel could not help praying. In his mind, not doing it would mean betraying his faith in God.

His enemies were watching closely, and they saw Daniel kneeling in prayer. At once they went back to the king.

"O King Darius, have you not made a law that if anyone offers a prayer, he shall be thrown into the den of lions?" they asked.

"It is true," said the king. "The law has been made, and it must stand."

"Yet there is a man who does not obey the law," they told him. "Every day, Daniel prays to his God three times."

"Not Daniel!" cried the king. "Then I will change the law."

"You cannot," his noblemen told him. "You made the law so that it could not be changed."

The king was heartbroken over what he had done, for he loved Daniel and knew that no one could take his place in the kingdom. All day, until the sun went down, he tried to find some way to save Daniel's life, but when evening came, the noblemen again reminded him that the law must be kept.

Very sadly the king sent for Daniel and gave an order that he should be thrown into the den of lions. "Perhaps your God, whom you serve so faithfully, will save you," Darius told him.

They led Daniel to the mouth of a great pit where the lions were kept and threw him in. Over the mouth of the pit they placed a great stone. The king sealed it with his seal so that no one would dare take away the stone and let Daniel out.

King Darius went to his palace, but he was so sad that he could not eat or listen to the music he loved. He could not sleep, for all through the night he was thinking of poor Daniel.

Early the next morning, he rose from his bed and hurried to the den of lions. He broke the seal and took away the stone. In a voice full of sorrow he called out, scarcely hoping to hear any answer except the roaring of the lions.

"O Daniel, has your God kept you safe?" he called.

And out of the darkness in the den came the voice of Daniel, saying, "O king, God has sent his angel to protect me, and has shut the mouths of the lions. They have not hurt me, because God saw that I had done no wrong. And I have done no wrong toward you, O king!"

The king looked down and saw Daniel standing in the pit among the hungry lions. They had not harmed him all night long, because he had trusted with all his heart that God would save him.

King Darius was overjoyed. He ordered his servants to take Daniel out of the den, and Daniel was brought out safe and sound. Then, by the king's command, the servants seized the noblemen who had plotted against Daniel and threw them into the pit. The hungry lions leapt upon them and tore them apart until nothing was left but their bones!

Then Darius sent a message out to all the people under his rule, saying that they all should honor God. "For he is the living God, and his kingdom shall have no end," he decreed.

Daniel was returned to his high office, and he kept his faith in the Lord.

What God Hath Promised

~ ANNIE JOHNSON FLINT

This is a good poem to remember when God gives us a cross to bear.

God hath not promised
   Skies always blue,
Flower-strewn pathways
   All our lives through.
God hath not promised
   Sun without rain,
Joy without sorrow,
   Peace without pain.

But God hath promised
   Strength for the day,
Rest for the labor,
   Light for the way,
Grace for the trials,
   Help from above,
Unfailing sympathy,
   Undying Love.

Where Love Is, God Is

☞ LEO TOLSTOY

Here is a good man who lives the Gospel.

In a little town in Russia there once lived a shoemaker named Martin. He had a tiny shop in the basement of a house. Through one little window he could look out and see the feet of those who passed by.

One night, when he had finished his work, Martin took the lamp, set it on a table, and sat down to read his Bible. He read about the man who invited the Lord to dinner at his house but did not treat him well. Martin took off his glasses, laid them on his Bible, and pondered.

"If the Lord came to my house, how would I behave?" he wondered. Then he put his head on both his arms, and before he knew it, fell asleep.

"Martin!" He suddenly heard a voice nearby.

He started from his sleep. "Who is there?" he asked.

He turned around and looked at the door, but no one was there. Then he heard the voice again: "Martin! Look out into the street tomorrow, for I shall come."

Martin rubbed his eyes, but he did not know whether he had heard the words in a dream or awake. He put out the lamp and lay down to sleep.

The next morning he rose early and said his prayers, and after breakfast he sat down by the window. He looked out into the street as he worked. Many different shoes trudged past.

Soon a man named Stephen came by. Martin knew him by his shabby boots. It was his job to shovel away the snow. The man was old and broken down. He had to stop and rest every few minutes, for he did not have much strength.

Martin went to the door and called him. "Come in and warm yourself a bit," he said. "I'm sure you must be cold."

"Bless you," Stephen answered. "My bones do ache, to be sure." He tottered inside and sat before the fire. As he drank warm tea, he noticed that Martin kept looking outside.

"Are you expecting anyone?" Stephen asked.

"No, not really," said Martin. "Well, you see, last night as I was reading my Bible, I began to doze, and I heard someone call me by name. Then I thought I heard someone whispering, 'Expect me. I will come tomorrow.' I am embarrassed to admit it, but now I keep looking for the dear Lord!"

Stephen finished his tea in silence, then rose to go. "Thank you, Martin," he said. "You have given me food and comfort for both body and soul." He went away, and Martin sat back down by the window to work.

Soon a woman passed by in her peasant shoes. Martin looked up through the window and saw that she was a stranger, poorly dressed, with a baby in her arms. Her clothes were ragged. She had hardly anything to wrap the baby in.

Martin went to the door and called her. "My dear! Come out of the cold. You can wrap your baby in a warm place." The woman was surprised to hear the shoemaker calling to her, but she followed him into the little room.

Martin led her to the fire, and he gave her some soup and bread. She looked so cold, and her dress was so thin.

While she ate, Martin went and looked among his things. He brought back a blanket. "Take it," he said. "It's a worn-out old thing, but it will do to wrap the baby."

"Bless you, friend," said the woman with tears in her eyes. After she had warmed herself, Martin saw her out.

After a while, an old woman came by with a sack of

apples on her back. She stopped to rest in front of the window, placing the sack on the ground. Just then a boy in a tattered cap ran up, snatched an apple out of the sack, and tried to slip away. But the woman saw him and caught him by the sleeve. She began pulling his hair, and the boy screamed. Martin rushed out of the door and ran into the street.

"Let me go!" the boy cried. "I didn't do anything."

Martin separated them. "Let him go, Granny. He won't do it again."

The old woman let go. The boy tried to run away, but Martin stopped him.

"Ask her forgiveness," he said firmly. "And don't do it another time. I saw you take the apple."

The boy began to cry and say he was sorry.

"That's right," said Martin. "Now here's an apple for you. I will pay you for it, Granny."

"I should take the rascal to the police!" the apple-woman yelled.

"He's just a boy," said Martin. "God tells us to forgive."

"That's true," sighed the old woman. "After all, it was only his childishness."

As she was about to hoist the sack on her back, the boy sprang forward, saying, "Let me carry it for you, Granny. I'm going that way." The old woman nodded and put the sack on his back, and they went down the street together.

When they were out of sight Martin went inside and sat down again to work. Soon it began to grow dark, so he lit his lamp and worked awhile longer. After he finished a boot, he gathered his tools and swept the floor. Then he placed the lamp on the table and took his Bible from the shelf.

As he opened it, yesterday's dream came back to his mind, and suddenly he thought he heard footsteps behind him. He turned around, and it seemed as if people were standing in the dark corner. A voice whispered, "Martin, don't you know me?"

"Who is it?" muttered Martin.

"It is I," said the voice. And out of the dark corner stepped Stephen, who smiled and then vanished like a cloud.

"It is I," said the voice again. And out of the darkness stepped the woman with the baby in her arms. The woman smiled and the baby laughed, and they also vanished.

"It is I," said the voice once more. The old woman and the boy with the apple stepped out. They both smiled, and they too vanished.

Martin's soul was glad. He put on his glasses and began reading the Bible. At the top of the page he read:

I was hungry, and you gave me meat. I was thirsty, and you gave me drink. I was a stranger, and you took me in.

A few verses later, he read:

As you did it to one of the least of these my brothers, you did it to me.

Then Martin understood that his dream had come true. The Savior had really come to him that day, and Martin had welcomed him.

11

The Captain's Daughter

JAMES T. FIELDS

When one person shows faith in God, it helps others to follow.

We were crowded in the cabin,
    Not a soul would dare to sleep.
It was midnight on the waters,
    And a storm was on the deep.

'Tis a fearful thing in winter
    To be shattered by the blast,
And to hear the rattling trumpet
    Thunder, "Cut away the mast!"

So we shuddered there in silence—
    For the strongest held his breath,
While the hungry sea was roaring
    And the breakers talked with Death.

As thus we sat in darkness,
    Each one busy with his prayers,
"We are lost!" the captain shouted
    As he staggered down the stairs.

But his little daughter whispered,
    As she took his icy hand,
"Isn't God upon the ocean,
    Just the same as on the land?"

Then we kissed the little maiden,
    And we spoke in better cheer,
And we anchored safe in harbor
    When the morn was shining clear.

In the Uttermost Parts of the Sea

HANS CHRISTIAN ANDERSEN

The title of this beautiful story comes from Psalm 139.
God is with us wherever we wander.

Some ships had been sent toward the North Pole to find out what was up there. Through ice and mist, they had steered farther and farther north. Now winter had begun. The sun had set, and the explorers would not see it again for a long time. One long night would continue for weeks and weeks.

A vast plain of ice spread around the ships, and the snow lay heaped on the frozen sea. The explorers made little houses shaped like domes out of the snow, just big enough for two or three of them to crawl inside. Overhead, nature's fireworks—the great Northern Lights—flashed red and blue in the dark sky.

Sometimes Eskimos came with sleds full of animal skins to trade. The explorers were glad to use the skins as beds to keep warm inside their snow houses, while outside it grew colder and colder. They knew that at home it was still autumn, and they thought of the sunbeams and the leaves still clinging to the trees in crimson and gold.

Their watches told them it was time for rest, and two of the men had already lain down to sleep. The younger had his greatest treasure with him, a Bible that his grandmother had given him. Every night it lay under his pillow. Every day he read from it, and as he lay in his bed he thought of these words which brought so much comfort: "If I take the wings of the morning, and dwell in the uttermost parts of

the sea, even there shall thy hand lead me, and thy right hand shall hold me."

These words of faith were on his lips as he closed his eyes and began to sleep. With sleep came dreams. First he seemed to hear songs he had loved at home. A mild summer breeze breathed upon him, and a light shone on his bed. He lifted his head and found that the dazzling white light was coming from the large wings of an angel looking down on him, an angel whose eyes beamed with love.

The angel seemed to rise from the pages of the Bible. He spread his arms, and the narrow walls of the snow hut disappeared like a mist melting before daylight. The green meadows and autumn woods of the young explorer's home lay around him instead, bathed in quiet sunshine. The stork's nest was empty, but the apples still clung to the wild apple tree. A little bird whistled in the cage that hung in the window of his home. It whistled the tune he had taught it, and his old grandmother was feeding it, just as he used to.

The blacksmith's pretty young daughter stood drawing

water from the well. As she nodded to the grandmother, the old woman called her, and held up a letter that had come that morning from the cold northern lands, from the North Pole itself, where the old woman's grandson was now, safe under God's protecting hand.

The two women, old and young, laughed and cried as they read the letter, and the young explorer who slept amid the ice and snow, his spirit roaming in the world of dreams, under the angel's wings, saw and heard it all, and laughed and cried with them. From the letter they read these words aloud: "Even in the uttermost parts of the sea . . . thy right hand shall hold me." The words seemed to come like sweet, solemn music, and the angel folded his wings. Like a soft protecting veil they fell close over the sleeper.

The dream was over. All was dark in the little snow hut, but the Bible lay under the young man's head, while faith and hope filled his heart. God was with him, and his home was with him, even in the uttermost parts of the sea.

The Legend
of Saint Christopher

*We should use our God-given strengths
in the service of God and our fellow travelers in life.*

Long ago there lived a man who was so tall and strong he seemed like a giant. He could carry almost any load, so people gave him the name Offero, which meant the Bearer. Offero was very proud of his strength, and he made up his mind to serve no one but the mightiest ruler in the world. He went to the castle of a very rich and powerful king.

"Great monarch!" said Offero. "I wish to serve only the mightiest king. Will you accept me?"

The king gladly took him into his castle, and Offero served him faithfully for many years. But one day he saw the king tremble at the name of Satan. Offero asked the king why he was afraid.

"I fear Satan because he is the Prince of Evil," said the king. "He rules the world, I am told."

"If you are afraid of him, he must be more powerful than you," Offero said scornfully. "I must find him, for I want to serve only the greatest of rulers."

So Offero set off to find his new master. He traveled many days until one afternoon he found himself in a dark forest. There, on a great stone, sat a shadow. It was the Prince of Evil.

"I am looking for the one who rules the world," Offero announced boldly.

"Good!" Satan laughed. "You have found him. Come with me, and I will keep you busy."

It was not pleasant work. It meant that every minute was spent making trouble for other people. But Offero did as he was told, because he believed he was serving the strongest king at last.

One day, as they traveled along, they came in sight of a small, rough-hewn cross by the side of the road. At once Satan left the path and went a long way around, over rocks and through bushes, and at last came back to the road with the cross well behind him.

"Why did you do that?" asked Offero, for Satan seldom made so much trouble for himself.

"I do not like to go near the cross," Satan admitted. "I fear him whose sign it is."

Offero's heart leapt with joy.

"What is his name?" he demanded.

"I dare not say his name," Satan answered, "but some call him the Prince of Peace."

"If you fear him, he must be stronger than you," Offero said. "I will leave you and serve him."

Once again he set out in search of this new master. He traveled far, for he did not know the way, but hope and courage never failed him. At last he found a man, an ancient hermit, who looked as if he might know how to find the Prince of Peace. Offero told him his story.

"I will serve him, if I can find him," he told the old man. "Where is he? I will kill all his enemies, if he wishes."

"That is not the way," the hermit said quietly. "This prince differs from all others. I will show you how to serve him."

He led Offero to the bank of a swift, wide river.

"Here many travelers have lost their lives, for no boat can survive these waters," he said. "If you will stand here on the bank, and carry people across, you will be serving the Prince of Peace. He will know of your service."

So Offero built a hut beside the river and cut a mighty

staff to guide his feet among the sunken rocks, and he waited for travelers to come along. They found him always at the door of his hut, ready to carry them across on his broad shoulders. Year after year he labored, and not one traveler was lost. It seemed strange to him that he should be serving this way. Sometimes he would sigh and wonder if the Prince of Peace really knew of his work. But the people he helped became his friends, and he was never really lonely.

One night there came a great storm of wind and rain. Offero lay down to sleep in his hut, for surely no travelers would be out on such a night. Yet as he closed his eyes, he heard a faint call.

"Offero! Will you take me over the river?"

He went to his door and looked outside, but he saw no one. He went back to his bed and lay down. Again he heard the voice.

"Offero! Bear me over the river!"

He grabbed his staff and went down to the riverbank. There he came upon a little child, who begged him, "Offero, Offero, carry me over the river tonight."

Offero knew the dangers of the river in such a storm, but the child was waiting for him. So he lifted him onto his shoulders, cried, "Hold tightly to me, little one," and slowly stepped into the water.

The current was swifter than ever before. As he plunged deeper and deeper into the river, his burden seemed to grow heavier and heavier, until he feared they would both sink. Each step was harder than the last. The water beat against him, and the wind roared in his ears. His great staff bent as he pushed forward, and the river had never seemed so wide. At last he reached the other side, tired and safe, and gently lifted the child from his shoulders.

"Who are you, my child?" he panted. "It felt as though I were carrying the weight of the whole world."

"Do you not know me?" the sweet voice answered. "I am the One you have promised to serve. Did you not know that in this humble, hard work of aiding so many weary travelers, you were serving me all along? And from now on you will be called not Offero, the Bearer, but Christopher, the Christ-bearer, for I have accepted you as my faithful servant."

Christopher fell to his knees and prayed in silence. When he opened his eyes, he was alone by the river. He rose, picked up his staff, and went back to his work of helping travelers for the rest of his days.

Morning Prayers

In the morning, prayer is the key that opens us to God's blessings.

I thank thee, Lord, for sleep and rest,
For all the things that I love best.
Now guide me through another day
And bless my work and bless my play.
                    Amen.

Father, help each little child,
Make us truthful, good, and mild,
Kind, obedient, modest, meek,
Mindful of the words we speak.

What is right may we pursue,
What is wrong refuse to do.
What is evil seek to shun,
This we ask for everyone.
                    Amen.

Let the words of my mouth, and the meditation
  of my heart, be acceptable in thy sight,
O Lord, my strength, and my redeemer.
Amen.

Dear Lord, of thee three things I pray:
To know thee more clearly,
To love thee more dearly,
To serve thee more nearly every day.
Amen.

The Healing
of the Paralytic

When we have faith, miracles can happen.
Here is the story of a man who is saved by the faith of his friends.

Jesus lived and taught for a while in Capernaum, a town by the Sea of Galilee. One day a crowd of people flocked to the house where he was staying so that they could hear his words. Soon the house was full of people. The crowd overflowed into the yard, and even into the streets.

Four men arrived, carrying a friend who lay on a mat. This man was very sick and could not move. His four friends quickly saw that they could not possibly bring their friend through the thick crowd. But they were so eager to

reach Jesus, they would not think of turning back. So they
did something clever and daring. They climbed to the top of
the house and lifted their friend with them. Then they went
to work pulling up pieces of the roof.

The people inside the house looked up, for all of a sudden light came streaming from overhead. Four faces peered
down at them from a hole in the roof. The faces disappeared, and four pairs of hands began lowering the sick
man into the house, ever so gently, right toward the place
where Jesus stood.

The crowd held its breath. Jesus smiled as he saw the
paralyzed man being let down on his mat. He knew that the
four men on the roof believed in him, and that they had no
doubt he could cure their friend. Because of their great
faith, he said to the paralyzed man, "Get up, take up your
mat, and go home."

Some of the people in the crowded house snickered. "Who does this Jesus think he is?" they whispered to themselves. "That fellow will never walk."

But suddenly they stopped whispering and stared with mouths hanging wide open. The sick man, who only a moment before could not even move, was stirring. And all at once he was well. He stood on his feet, picked up the mat on which he had been lying, and walked out through the crowd, which opened to make a path for him.

"Praise God!" the people cried. "We have never seen anything like this before!" And so the news of Jesus' teaching and works of healing continued to spread.

The Call of Samuel

We may not hear God's voice with our ears, but we can hear it in our hearts.
We must be ready to answer his call, as Samuel did:
"Speak, Lord, for your servant hears you."

Once there was a woman named Hannah who lived in a hilly country called Ephraim. Hannah had many blessings to be thankful for. She had a good home and a kind husband named Elkanah. They had fields of wheat, vineyards of grapes, and great flocks of sheep.

There was one thing they did not have, though. They had no children. Hannah loved children very much, for she knew that they are the greatest blessing of all. It made her sad to think that their house was so empty and still, and that there were no voices of boys or girls in it.

Those were the days when people were beginning to learn that all good things are given by God. Hannah knew this too, and she prayed that God would give her a child. After a while, God sent a little son to Hannah and Elkanah. They named him Samuel and loved him very much because he had come in answer to his mother's prayer.

Soon Samuel grew from a baby to a little boy. He was good and strong and always a comfort to his mother and father.

One year, when Samuel was still a boy, Hannah decided that it was time for him to learn how to serve the Lord. So she took him to the temple at Shiloh to be trained as a priest. Her heart ached at parting from her son, but she knew that he would learn wonderful things by living in God's house for a while. She gave him a little coat to wear, and every year when she came to visit, she brought him a larger one that she had made with her own hands.

The temple was a great, still place. It was very different from Samuel's home in the hills with its vines and flowering trees. But the chief priest, a man named Eli, was a kind man. He took good care of Samuel and taught him to obey God's law.

Eli became very old, and his eyes grew so dim that he could barely see. Samuel found all kinds of ways to help him with his duties. In the temple was a lamp that was lit every evening. It was Samuel's job to keep it burning through the night. He kept watch over the lamp and slept in the great temple.

It was a lonely place for a boy to stay at night. It was very quiet and dark, except for the light of the lamp. The tall stone pillars cast long shadows on the floor, which trembled and seemed almost alive. Samuel could be very brave and not miss his mother too much in the daytime, when the sun shone and everything was bright. But at night he was like any other child. Sometimes he was afraid of the dark.

One night, as Samuel lay in his bed, he was startled to hear a voice calling him. "Samuel! Samuel!" called the voice.

"Here I am!" Samuel answered. He jumped up and ran to Eli. "Here I am," he said. "You called me."

"I did not call you, Samuel," said the old man. "Lie down again."

So Samuel went and lay down, but soon he heard the voice calling him again.

"Samuel! Samuel!"

Samuel again ran to Eli and woke him. "Here I am," he said. "You called me."

Eli said, "I did not call you. Lie down again."

Samuel went back into the dark temple and lay down, and tried to go to sleep, but a third time he heard the voice calling him.

"Samuel! Samuel!"

"Eli, Eli, here I am. You did call me!" he cried as he ran again into the old priest's room.

This time Eli understood that it had been the voice of God speaking to Samuel. He said to the little boy, "Go lie down, and if he calls you, then you must answer, 'Speak, Lord, for your servant hears you.'" So Samuel went and lay down in his bed.

God called once more, "Samuel! Samuel!"

Samuel answered bravely, as Eli had told him to do,

"Speak, Lord, for your servant hears you." Then God talked to Samuel a long time in the temple, telling him many wonderful things.

Samuel listened carefully. After the voice had stopped speaking, he no longer felt afraid or lonely. Now he knew that he was never alone, for God was with him, even in the dark. He slept without fear until it was morning and time to open the doors of the house of the Lord.

Samuel grew up to be brave and good, just as his mother had hoped. He became a very wise man, for God spoke to him often, and he was known far and wide as a great prophet.

The Boy and the Angel

God hears each and every one of us.
This story is based on a poem by the great English poet Robert Browning.

Though he was only a boy, Theocrite had to earn his living. He swept floors, and washed dishes, and carried firewood. His days were long and his work was hard, but his spirit was strong and he was forever singing.

"Praise God!" sang Theocrite. Morning, noon, and night he sang at his work. His cheerful song brought joy to his own heart and to the hearts of everyone around him. And it brought joy to God, who heard him from on high.

One day, as Theocrite was singing at his work, a monk passed by. He was so touched by the song's sweetness and charm that he stopped to listen for a while.

"Well done, my son," said the monk. "I have no doubt that God hears your praise. I'm sure it pleases him just as much as if you were the pope in St. Peter's Church at Rome, singing the glad hymns at Easter time."

Theocrite was happy in his work, but the thought of singing in the great cathedral in Rome made his face light up. "I wish that I might praise God in St. Peter's Church before I die!" he said.

Now, the angel Gabriel happened to overhear his wish.

"What an excellent idea," he told himself. "Theocrite's song of praise is so pleasing, he would make a wonderful pope someday."

The very next morning, Theocrite was gone from his usual place. The angel had carried him away to Rome so that he might grow up to become the new pope and sing his songs in St. Peter's Church!

But soon God said, "Why is it that I do not hear the voice of little Theocrite singing at his work?"

At that, the angel Gabriel spread his wings and sank to the earth. He became a boy like Theocrite, taking his place as best as he could. He could do the boy's work easily enough, and he tried to sing his song of praise as well. But he could not.

"I hear a voice of praise, but it is too perfect," said God. "It is not the same as the song of Theocrite. I miss my little human voice."

Then the angel Gabriel cast off his disguise. No one can really replace another, and even the angel found that he could not entirely fill the place of the little boy.

Gabriel flew to Rome and paused above the dome at St.

Peter's Church. Theocrite was now grown into a man, and he was the new pope. It was Easter time, and he was about to praise God in the great cathedral.

"I took you from your trade, and made you the pope in Rome," Gabriel told him, "but it was all a mistake. I did not do well. You could be a great pope, but no one can take your place in your old home.

"I left my angel sphere to do your work," he explained. "Your voice seemed so weak to me, but I could not take up your song.

"All the voices of earth rise as a wondrous chorus to the ear of God. Without you the great chorus was not the same. He missed your little song of praise.

"Come back with me to your old home and your old work, Theocrite. Come back to your boyhood and sing your praises to God again."

And so Theocrite went back to being a little boy who sang happily as he worked, and he grew old at home. He never sang the praises of God in St. Peter's Church in Rome. But many years later, when he and the new pope came to die, they went to heaven side by side.

The Little Lost Lamb

In God's eyes, everyone counts. This story is based on Luke 15:3–7.

The little lamb was the youngest one in the flock.

It was a tiny lamb with a thin coat of wool and slender legs. At night it slept in the sheepfold close to its mother's warm fleece. All day long it nibbled grass, and drank from a running stream, and played in the meadow.

"Take care of me," the little lamb tried to say to the shepherd of the flock. "I am too little and weak to take care of myself."

The shepherd understood, and he watched over the little lamb although there were a hundred sheep in his flock.

He was a good shepherd or he would not have been able to care for them all. Every morning he opened the gate of the fold and they crowded out. Then he led them up a hill to a green meadow, where he watched them all day. There were wolves in the mountains close by, watching for a chance to kill the little lambs. The shepherd kept the wolves away.

When the sun began to drop down behind the hill, the shepherd led his flock to the fold. And before he closed the gate, he always counted the flock to see if there were a hundred sheep.

A storm in a high place is very terrible. One day there was a storm with wind, and cold rain, and fire in the sky. The sheep were too frightened to know which way to go. They bleated and pushed and almost crushed each other as they ran down the hill. But the shepherd led them all gently, pointing the way with his crook. He called them by the names he had given them. He went first to keep the storm from beating them back. At last the sheepfold was in sight.

As they went through the gate, one by one, he counted them.

There were only ninety-nine.

The shepherd looked down at the trembling sheep. He knew right away which one was lost in the storm.

If he had not been a good shepherd, he might have thought that so little a lamb was no great loss. But he thought only about how cold the lamb must be with its thin fleece, out in the storm. He remembered that, above the storm, he had heard the howling of wolves.

So the good shepherd went out in the wind and rain to find the little lamb.

It had grown so dark that he could hardly see. The wind was cold, the rain soaked his cloak, and the stones cut his feet. Another shepherd would have turned back. But the good shepherd had promised to take care of the little lamb. So he went on until he found it, lying so cold and frightened beside the road.

The shepherd took the lamb in his arms. It was too cold to walk home. All the way back he carried it, just as carefully as your mother carried you when you were a baby. He was very happy when he reached the sheepfold. He asked his neighbors to come and be glad with him because not even one lamb was lost from the flock.

They wondered a little that the shepherd was so glad.

"Ninety-nine is almost a hundred," they said. "What difference would one little lamb have made in so large a flock?"

The good shepherd knew. The little lamb who was lost was one of his sheep, and he loved them all.

The Twenty-third Psalm

We belong to God, and he will take care of us.

The Lord is my shepherd; I shall not want.

He maketh me to lie down in green pastures: he leadeth
me beside the still waters.

He restoreth my soul: he leadeth me in the paths of
righteousness for his name's sake.

Yea, though I walk through the valley of the shadow of
death, I will fear no evil: for thou art with me; thy rod
and thy staff they comfort me.

Thou preparest a table before me in the presence of mine
enemies: thou anointest my head with oil;
my cup runneth over.

Surely goodness and mercy shall follow me all the days of
my life: and I will dwell in the house of the Lord for ever.

The Selfish Giant

☞ OSCAR WILDE

*Suffer the little children to come unto me, and forbid them not:
for of such is the kingdom of God.* — MARK 10:14

Every afternoon, as they were coming from school, the children used to go and play in the Giant's garden. It was a large lovely garden with soft green grass, beautiful flowers, and twelve peach trees with blossoms of pink and pearl. "How happy we are!" the children cried to each other.

One day the Giant came back. He had been to visit his friend the Ogre, and had been gone for seven years. When he arrived, he saw the children playing in the garden.

"What are you doing here?" he cried in a very gruff voice, and the children ran away.

"This garden is mine," said the Giant. "Nobody can play in it but me." He built a high wall around it, and put up a sign: *Trespassers Will Be Prosecuted.* He was a very selfish Giant.

Then the poor children had nowhere to play. They used to wander around the high walls and talk about the beautiful garden inside. "How happy we were there!" they said.

Then the Spring came, and all over the country there were little blossoms and little birds. Only in the garden of the Selfish Giant it was still winter. The birds did not care to sing in it as there were no children, and the trees forgot to blossom. The only people who were pleased with it were the Snow and the Frost. "Spring has forgotten his garden," they cried, "so we will live here all the year around." The Snow covered up the grass with her great white cloak, and the Frost painted all the trees silver. They invited the North Wind and the Hail to stay with them, too.

"I cannot understand why the Spring is so late in coming," said the Selfish Giant. "I hope there will be a change in the weather."

But the Spring never came, nor the Summer nor Autumn. "He is too selfish," they said. So it was always Winter there, and the North Wind and the Hail and the Frost and the Snow danced about through the trees.

One morning the Giant was lying awake in bed when he heard some lovely music. It was only a little bird singing outside his window, but it was so long since he had heard one sing in his garden that it seemed to him to be the most beautiful music in the world. Then the Hail stopped dancing over his head, and the North Wind ceased roaring. "I believe the Spring has come at last," said the Giant, and he jumped out of bed and looked out.

What did he see?

He saw a most wonderful sight. Through a little hole in the wall the children had crept in, and they were sitting in the branches of the trees. The trees were so glad to have the children back again that they had covered themselves with blossoms. The birds were flying about, and the flowers were looking up through the green grass and laughing. It was a lovely scene, only in one corner it was still winter. It was the farthest corner of the garden, and in it was standing a little boy. He was so small that he could not reach up to the branches of the tree, and he was wandering all around it, crying bitterly. The poor tree was still covered with frost and snow.

The Giant's heart melted as he looked out. "How selfish I have been!" he said. "Now I know why Spring would not come here. I will put that poor little boy on the top of the tree, and then I will knock down the wall, and my garden shall be the children's playground for ever." He was really very sorry for what he had done.

So he crept downstairs and went out into the garden. But when the children saw him they were so frightened that they all ran away, and the garden became winter again. Only the little boy did not run, for his eyes were so full of tears he did not see the Giant coming.

The Giant took him gently in his hand and put him up into the tree. And the tree broke at once into blossom, and the birds came and sang on it, and the little boy flung his arms around the Giant's neck, and kissed him.

The other children, when they saw that the Giant was not wicked any longer, came running back, and with them came the Spring. "It is your garden now, little children," said the Giant, and he took a great ax and knocked down the wall.

All day long the children played, and in the evening they bid the Giant goodbye.

"But where is your little companion?" he said. "The boy I put into the tree."

"We don't know," answered the children. "He has gone away."

"You must tell him to be sure and come tomorrow," said the Giant. But the children said they did not know where he lived and had never seen him before, and the Giant felt very sad.

Every afternoon, when school was over, the children came and played with the Giant. But the little boy whom the Giant loved was never seen again. The Giant longed for his little friend. "How I would like to see him!" he used to say.

Years went by, and the Giant grew very old and feeble. He could not play anymore, so he sat in a huge armchair and watched the children at their games, and admired his garden. "I have many beautiful flowers," he said. "But the children are the most beautiful flowers of all."

One winter morning he looked out of his window as he was dressing. He did not hate the Winter now, for he knew that it was merely the Spring asleep, and that the flowers were resting.

Suddenly he saw a marvelous sight. In the farthest corner of the garden was a tree covered with white blossoms. Its branches were golden, and silver fruit hung down from them, and underneath it stood the little boy he had loved.

The Giant ran out into the garden with great joy. He hastened across the grass, and came near the child. When he came quite close his face grew red with anger, and he said, "Who hath dared to wound thee?" For on the palms of the child's hands were the prints of two nails, and the prints of two nails were on the little feet.

"Who hath dared to wound thee?" cried the Giant. "Tell me, that I may take my big sword and slay him."

"Nay," answered the child. "But these are the wounds of Love."

"Who art thou?" said the Giant, and a strange awe fell on him, and he knelt before the little child.

The child smiled on the Giant, and said to him, "You let me play once in your garden. Today you shall come with me to my garden, which is Paradise."

And when the children ran in that afternoon, they found the Giant lying dead under the tree, all covered with white blossoms.

Babouscka

Edith M. Thomas

*In Russia, Babouscka is said to leave presents in the houses of good children
on Christmas Eve. This old tale reminds us that whenever a chance to serve
God comes along, we should take it.*

Babouscka sits before the fire,
　　Upon a winter's night.
The driving winds heap up the snow,
　　Her hut is snug and tight.
The howling winds, they only make
　　Babouscka's fire more bright!

She hears a knocking at the door,
　　So late—who can it be?
She hastes to lift the wooden latch
　　(No thought of fear has she).
The wind-blown candle in her hand
　　Shines out on strangers three.

Their beards are white with age and snow
　　That in the darkness flies.
Their floating locks are long and white,
　　But kindly are the eyes
That sparkle underneath their brows,
　　Like stars in frosty skies.

"Babouscka, we have come from far.
　　We tarry but to say,
A little Prince is born this night
　　Who all the world shall sway.
Come join the search. Come, go with us
　　Who go these gifts to pay."

50

Babouscka shivers at the door:
  "I would I might behold
The little Prince who shall be King,
  But ah, the night is cold,
The wind so fierce, the snow so deep,
  And I, good sirs, am old!"

The strangers three, no word they speak,
  But fade in snowy space.
Babouscka sits before the fire,
  And looks with wistful face.
"I wish that I had questioned them,
  So I the way might trace!

"When morning comes, with blessed light,
  I'll early be awake.
My staff in hand, I'll go—perchance,
  Those strangers overtake.
And for the Child, some little toys
  I'll carry for His sake."

The morning came, and, staff in hand,
  She wandered in the snow,
And asked the way of all she met,
  But none the way could show.
"It must be farther yet," she sighed,
  "Then farther will I go."

And still 'tis said, on Christmas Eve,
  When high the drifts are piled,
With staff and basket on her arm,
  Babouscka seeks the Child.
At every door her face is seen,
  Her wistful face and mild!

At every door her gifts she leaves,
  And bends, and murmurs low,
Above each little face half hid
  by pillows white as snow:
"And is He here?"—then softly sighs:
  "Nay, farther I must go!"

Prayers of Thanks

In every thing give thanks. —I THESSALONIANS 5:18

God is great, God is good,
Let us thank him for this food.
By his hand we all are fed
Give us, Lord, our daily bread.
                    Amen.

All good things around us
Are sent from heaven above.
Then thank the Lord, O thank the Lord
For all his love.
                    Amen.

Thank you, Father, for our homes,
For our parents kind and true,
Most of all for thy dear Son,
May we try his will to do.
                    Amen.

Bless us, O Lord, and these, thy gifts,
Which we are about to receive from thy bounty,
Through Christ our Lord.
                    Amen.

Ben Franklin's Reminder

Many of the men and women who founded this country believed that without God's blessing, the United States would never have come into being.

The time was long ago, in the year 1787. A terrible war was finally over. Americans had won their freedom from the king of England. Now they could make their own rules and choose their own leaders.

Men like George Washington, James Madison, and Benjamin Franklin gathered in the city of Philadelphia, where they faced the job of building a new country. Together they hoped to come up with a plan for how Americans would live with each other. It would not be an easy task.

Day after day they met at Independence Hall and talked. Outside, the sun blazed in the summer sky, and inside, tempers grew hot. The talk turned into arguments about how to form a government. The men began to throw angry speeches and unkind words at one another. Sometimes they glared and used bitter tones. A few gave up and went home in disgust. Others let it be known that they were ready to quit.

George Washington looked on in despair. The country was brand new, and already it was about to fall apart. All the long years of war, all the blood that had been shed for freedom would come to nothing. The mood of many was dark. Americans, it seemed, were not ready to trust one another. It would take a miracle to hold the young country together.

Then Ben Franklin rose from his seat. He was an old man and had hardly uttered a word in days. All eyes turned toward him as he began to speak.

He rose to remind them of something important. For weeks, they had been bickering and searching for answers. They were not likely to find those answers on their own, he said. They needed God's help.

"At the beginning of the war with England, when we were most aware of danger, we asked for God's protection," Ben Franklin told them. "Our prayers were answered. Now God has given us the chance to meet together and plan for the future of our country. Have we forgotten our powerful Friend? Or do we think we no longer need his help?"

Dead silence filled the room.

"I have lived a long time," he went on, "and the longer I live, the more proof I see of this truth: God governs in the affairs of men. If a sparrow cannot fall to the ground without his notice, can an empire rise without his aid? Without God's help, we will do no better than those who built the Tower of Babel. We will end up divided by our own selfishness, and our work will come to nothing."

The old man sat down. George Washington slowly nodded. When the members of the convention went back to their inns for the night, no doubt they thought about what had been said. Most of them were men of faith. Ben Franklin had reminded them to think on their duty and pray for strength. He was right—they needed God's wisdom more than ever.

Then a kind of miracle did happen. In the following days and weeks, the angry words slowly disappeared. The bitter arguing dried up. Instead, these men worked together to find some rules that Americans could use to govern themselves.

Those who met long ago in Philadelphia wanted the United States to be a good country. They struggled to make it a land where people could live in peace with one another and treat each other fairly. With much work, they wrote a set of basic laws for all Americans. They called it the Constitution. It still works for us today, and it helps us try to make America a place that pleases God.

Advice from
Thomas Jefferson

*A friend once asked Thomas Jefferson to give some advice to his young son.
Here is part of what Jefferson wrote.*

Adore God.

Reverence and cherish your parents.

Love your neighbor as yourself, and your country more
    than yourself.

Be just. Be true.

Murmur not at the ways of Providence.

So shall the life into which you have entered,
    be the portal to one of eternal and ineffable bliss.

The Story of "Amazing Grace"

God gives us his love, even when we do not deserve it. When we love him back, it changes our lives. It breaks the power of sin and frees us to do good.

John Newton threw his arms around a rail and hung on for life. Giant waves crashed across the deck, nearly dragging him overboard. The wind shrieked and tore at the ragged sails. The ship gave an awful groan, as if it were about to slide beneath the foaming water.

As he clung to the rail, John thought about the kind of life he had led. He knew that he had been a wicked, unkind man. He rarely saw anything good about the world, but had eyes for only the bad. All of his life he had lied to his friends, run away from duty, and made fun of God.

John was a sailor in the slave trade. It was an awful, cruel business. The sailors took men, women, and children from Africa, threw them in chains, and carried them away to America to be sold into bondage. John had never cared what happened to the slaves. He thought only about himself.

Now the terrible storm roared out of the black night. The ocean boiled, and cruel streaks of lightning ripped across the sky. A mountain of water thundered down on John's vessel, spun it around, and smashed a hole in its side.

The sailors ran to the pumps and tried to keep the sea out, but the water kept gaining. The ship lurched through the great swells. *We're going to sink*, John thought. *We're all going to drown*.

A sudden thought sprang to his mind, something his mother had taught him when he was just a boy. "God loves you," she had told him. "Have faith in him." *Could God really love someone like me?* John wondered. Gasping for breath, he cried into the wind: "Lord, have mercy upon us."

The ship pitched wildly, but it did not sink. Gradually the great swells calmed. The winds fell off, and the clouds began to break apart. Looking up at the stars, John could not help asking himself: *Why would God save a wretch like me? Perhaps there is something he wants me to do.*

As the years passed, John thought more and more about the storm. He knew the Lord was calling him to be a better man. So he gave up his life at sea, went home to England, and gave himself to the service of God by becoming a minister.

He could never forget his past, though. He thought about the slaves he had carried across the ocean in chains, and he was sorry for his sin. "How can I help put things right?" he prayed. John knew that he could not bring back all the poor people sold into bondage, but he could try to make sure that no more English ships would carry slaves. He began to speak out with others against the terrible practice. With God's aid he worked hard, and at last England passed a law putting a stop to its slave trade.

To the end of his days, John Newton's heart was full of wonder that God had saved him from his wicked ways. He knew that God loved him. He wrote this hymn in thanks and praise, and today it is loved all over the world.

Amazing grace, how sweet the sound,
That saved a wretch like me!
I once was lost, but now am found,
Was blind, but now I see.

'Twas grace that taught my heart to fear,
And grace my fears relieved,
How precious did that grace appear
The hour I first believed!

Through many dangers, toils and snares,
I have already come;
'Tis grace that brought me safe thus far,
And grace will lead me home.

The Lord has promised good to me,
His word my hope secures.
He will my shield and portion be
As long as life endures.

The Angel
of the Battlefield

*Our faith helps us take care of others, especially in times of trouble.
It gives us the strength to do what seems impossible.*

Clara Barton stood in front of the class. It was her first day as a teacher, and try as she might, she could not keep her hands from shaking. Every boy and girl in the room stared hard at her. She gazed back, numb with fright.

Some of the boys were bigger than Clara. A few were bullies who liked to be mean to teachers. All sorts of thoughts went whirling through Clara's mind. How was she to begin?

Her eyes fell on a Bible lying on her desk. Suddenly the doubt and fear fled. She picked up the book and asked the students to take turns reading.

"Blessed are the merciful, for they shall obtain mercy. Blessed are the pure in heart, for they shall see God." The children's faces began to soften as they listened.

"Why do you think Jesus said to love your enemies?" Clara asked. It was a hard question. The children were silent. At last one little girl raised her hand.

"I think it means that you must be good to everybody, and you mustn't quarrel or make anyone feel bad, and I'm going to try," she said.

Clara smiled, and her students smiled back. They knew that she would make a good teacher. She taught them to read and write, and helped them learn how to be good. Before long, even the big boys were glad to help her by cleaning the blackboards and carrying her books.

Many years passed. Then a bloody war came, the Civil War. Americans took up arms against each other, and the country saw terrible fighting.

Clara longed to help the sick and wounded soldiers. She went to the generals and begged them to let her go to the battlefields, where she could do the most good. They only shook their heads.

"The battlefield is no place for a woman," they told her. "It's too dangerous."

"Not for me," Clara replied.

Finally, after much pleading, the generals gave in. Clara found a wagon, loaded it with supplies, and headed for the front lines. Many of the soldiers had little to eat or wear. Clara gave them bread and water. She found shoes and clean shirts. She brought bandages to dress their wounds.

Clara nursed the injured men as the battles raged. Guns
blazed and cannons roared. Shells whistled through the air
and burst overhead. The soldiers gaped at the little woman
who moved among them, tying bandages and handing out
blankets.

One day Clara came across a young soldier lying on the
ground with a wounded arm. Half his shirt had been torn
away, and he trembled with cold and fear. As she stooped to
help, he flung his good arm around her neck and buried his
face in her skirt.

"Don't you know me?" he cried. "I used to carry your
books home from school."

Clara took the dirty face in her hands and recognized one
of her former pupils. "Why, Charlie, of course I remember
you," she said. "Don't worry, I'm here."

Somehow she was always there for the soldiers. She

brought clothes, soup, medicine, or whatever they needed most. She never seemed to rest. After a while, the grateful men began to call her the Angel of the Battlefield.

Finally the long war ended, but Clara still had much work to do. She knew that in times of great trouble, people would always need help. And so she did something wonderful. She worked hard to collect all sorts of things people might need in bad times—clothes, blankets, lanterns, medicine, pots for cooking, tools for building. Then she stored them all in big houses so they would be ready at a moment's notice. She found nurses and doctors who promised to help when they were needed too. It took a long time to organize so many people and supplies, but Clara refused to give up.

This was the beginning of the American Red Cross, which became part of the International Red Cross. Now Americans would have a way to aid one another quickly whenever disaster struck.

When a forest fire broke out in Michigan, the Red Cross rushed to help families whose homes had gone up in flames. When floods struck the Ohio River, Clara Barton and her friends were there, sailing up and down the swollen streams, handing out food and clothes to people who had lost everything to the waters. When an awful hurricane swept through South Carolina and no one else came forward to help, the Red Cross stepped up to the job.

In times of wars, disease, and hunger, Clara Barton was there, living in tents and bringing what relief she could. She never gave up. She always found a way. Even when she was an old woman, she went on working for others.

One day someone asked Clara how she kept the strength to help so many people. She repeated the words of Jesus: "Inasmuch as you have done it unto one of the least of these my brothers, you have done it unto me." She said, "I never did a day's work that was not built on that one little sentence."

Clara Barton died in 1912, but the work of the American Red Cross continues. Today it brings aid to millions of people. Red Cross volunteers help take care of our soldiers when they must fight overseas. They get blood to people who are sick or hurt, and help families when tornadoes, floods, and earthquakes strike. They even help children learn how to swim and be safe around the water.

From little seeds of faith, mighty works often grow. When you hear about the American Red Cross at work, you can remember that it all began with just one woman who drew strength from God to help so many others.

A Light to Guide Us

Thy word is a lamp unto my feet, and a light unto my path. —PSALM 119:105

One night a little girl and her father were walking down a country road together. It was the kind of night when the moon and stars hide behind the clouds. The girl carried a flashlight that lit up the road at their feet as they walked along, but beyond its glow, all was black. Sometimes the dark shapes of trees and bushes loomed along the road. Sometimes there was nothing but the emptiness of fields.

"I'm afraid," said the little girl.

"Why?" her father asked.

"Because the light only shows a little way ahead," she answered. "Everything else is dark."

"Yes, that's true," said her father. "But if we keep walking, the light will stay with us and help us see where we're going, all the way to the end of our journey."

And sure enough, the light kept them on the road. Little by little, step by step, it showed them the way until they reached home safe and sound.

Our faith is like a light we can carry with us. It gives us courage and helps us find our way in life. It does not show us everything we want to know, but it takes us forward, one step at a time. When we have faith, we may be able to see only a short distance ahead, but we also know that God will give us enough light for the whole journey.

The Boy Who Brought Light
into a World of Darkness

*Louis Braille refused to rest until he found a way
for blind people to read and write. His faith, courage, and hard work
changed millions of lives all over the world.*

More than anything else, young Louis Braille wanted to read. He longed to open book after book and know all the wonderful stories inside. But Louis had been blind since he was three years old. He could not see the blue sky, or the green grass, or the letters on the page of a book. He lived in a world of darkness.

Everyone in the little village of Coupvray watched out for the little blind boy. They listened for the tap of his cane and smiled when they saw him coming. They stopped their own work to guide him across the street or around a corner. They helped him count how many taps it took to get to the marketplace or the edge of town.

Often Louis would sit and talk with the kind village priest in his garden. Father Palluy read stories from the Bible and talked to Louis about how to be brave.

"Why did God have to make me blind?" Louis would ask.

"I do not know," Father Palluy answered, "but you must have faith. I believe that God has something special for you to do in life."

In those long-ago days, blind children were not allowed to go to school like other girls and boys. Father Palluy went to talk to the schoolmaster.

"Louis is a bright boy," he said. "He learns quickly. You should give him a chance."

"But if he cannot see the books, he cannot read," protested the schoolmaster. "How will he keep up?"

"Give him a chance," answered Father Palluy. "He will find a way."

So Louis went to school with the other boys and girls in the village. He listened closely to the teacher, and his classmates took turns reading to him. He seemed to remember everything, and soon he was at the top of his class.

Still, he was not really happy with his studies. He wanted to be able to read books and write letters like his classmates.

One day Father Palluy brought important news. "There is a school for blind children in the city of Paris," he said. "It has a special kind of book that blind people can read." Louis could hardly believe his ears. He begged his parents to send him to the wonderful school, and the priest helped them find money to pay the fees.

And so when he was ten years old, Louis and his father traveled to Paris, where the boy began school at the National Institute for the Young Blind. As soon as he arrived, he asked his new teachers the question that was burning in his mind: "Can you teach me to read?"

The teachers had made some books with big, raised let-

ters on the pages. By feeling the letters with their fingers, blind students could make out words and sentences. It was a clumsy, slow way to read, however. Louis was disappointed.

He studied as hard as he could, though, and learned quickly in his new school. He especially loved music, and he learned to play the organ. With his keen hearing, quick fingers, and sharp memory, he became a good musician. He spent hours at the organ in the nearby church, playing hymns and sacred music.

As the years went by, he kept wondering if there could be a better way for blind people to read, and even to write. Sometimes he lay awake at night, thinking over the problem again and again. He remembered some words that Father Palluy had read to him from the Bible: "Let there be light." Surely God wanted the light of knowledge to shine for everyone.

"Please, God," Louis prayed, "help me find a way for blind people to read and write."

He kept thinking, and trying, and testing different ideas. None of them worked. "You're wasting your time with these daydreams," some of his friends told him. "You're hoping for the impossible." But Louis had promised God that he would never give up.

Then one day Louis learned of a system worked out by a French army officer that used raised dots and dashes on paper to let soldiers send messages at night. An idea leapt into his mind. Maybe that kind of writing could help blind people read. "What if I make tiny patterns of raised dots on a page to stand for the letters?" Louis asked himself.

Hurrying to his room, he punched little holes in a piece of paper with a small pointed stick. Then he turned the paper over and ran his fingers over the bumps.

"This is it!" he cried. "If the patterns are small enough, the fingers can read quickly. Now I need a different pattern for each letter."

Month after month he worked. He would stay up late at night, searching and testing new patterns, until he fell asleep among his tools and papers. At last he had a code for each letter in the alphabet.

"Now," he told himself, "we'll see if it works." He punched a string of letters and then read aloud as he ran his fingers over the bumps: "My name is Louis Braille."

He fell to his knees and bowed his head. "Thank you, Lord, for answering my prayers," he whispered. "Now there will be a touch of light for those who live in a world of darkness."

Louis worked for years to improve his method. News of his idea slowly spread from country to country. All over the world, blind people began using Louis Braille's raised-dot system to read and write and learn. At last books could become part of their lives, all because a young boy kept the faith and devoted his life to finding a way. He opened the doors of knowledge to those who cannot see.

Saint Martin's Cloak

*This famous story about Martin of Tours, a patron saint of France,
takes place in the days of the Roman Empire.
It reminds us that God wants us to share with one another.*

It was a snowy, freezing day in the town of Amiens,
France. The winter winds blew hard, and icicles hung from
the trees. Little crowds of people bustled through the
marketplace, and the streets were filled with the sound of
their footsteps crunching across the hard-packed snow.
Shopkeepers stood in their doorways calling to one another.
A young scholar passed by, looking lost in thought, then a
servant girl searching for her mistress, then a rich mer-
chant hurrying home. Everyone was bundled up against the
bitter cold.

Beside a gate in the city wall stood a poor, ragged beggar. He had almost nothing to wear. Shivering with cold, he
held out a feeble hand to plead for alms. No one paid any
attention. They passed by without giving him a look. Some
even moved to the other side of the street so they would not
have to walk near him.

Suddenly the clopping of horses' hooves came echoing down the road. The emperor's soldiers were returning to town after riding about the walls of the city. They laughed and joked among themselves, and tossed proud glances at the people who paused to watch them ride by.

As they passed through the city gate, the trembling beggar stretched out his hand. The soldiers rode past him, thinking of the warm fires that awaited them back at their barracks. Only one—a young soldier named Martin—reined in his horse. A shadow of sadness came over his face when he noticed the poor, freezing beggar. He could not miss the despair in the man's eyes.

As Martin watched his comrades ride by, he wondered how he could help. There was no money in his purse, but he felt he must do something.

Then an idea sprang into his mind. He loosened the great, warm military cloak hanging from his shoulders and held it up with one hand. With the other hand he drew his sword and cut the cloth right down the middle. He leaned from the saddle and with a word of kindness dropped one half of the garment over the shoulders of the beggar. Then he sheathed his sword, tossed the rest of the cloak over his own shoulders, and galloped after his companions.

Some of the young officers laughed at Martin as he joined them with the torn cloak dangling over his back. But others wished they had thought of doing what he had done.

That night Martin had a dream. In it he saw Jesus in heaven, surrounded by a company of angels, and the Savior was wearing one half of a Roman soldier's cloak.

"Master, why are you wearing a torn cloak?" one of the angels asked. "Who gave it to you?"

And Jesus answered gently, "This is the garment Martin gave me."

Make Me an Instrument
of Your Peace

As this prayer reminds us, faith means doing.
It means doing God's will.

Lord, make me an instrument of your peace.
Where there is hatred, let me sow love;
Where there is injury, pardon;
Where there is doubt, faith;
Where there is despair, hope;
Where there is darkness, light;
And where there is sadness, joy.

O Divine Master, grant that I may not so much
    seek to be consoled as to console;
To be understood as to understand;
To be loved as to love.
For it is in giving that we receive;
It is in pardoning that we are pardoned;
It is in dying that we are born again
    to eternal life.

Miriam and the Floating Basket

The Book of Exodus tells how Moses led the Hebrew people out of bondage in Egypt. It begins with a wonderful story about a young girl who rescues her baby brother. Sometimes God calls on us to be very brave. Our faith gives us the courage we need.

This story takes place many, many years ago, when the Hebrew people lived in the land of Egypt. In those days the Hebrews were slaves of the king of Egypt, who was called Pharaoh. From morning until night, they toiled hard for Pharaoh, plowing the soil, digging ditches, making bricks, and building great temples. It was backbreaking work, and the Hebrew people suffered much.

Day after day, Pharaoh stood at his palace window watching the Hebrews labor under the hot sun. Even though their lives were hard, they kept growing in numbers and strength, and that frightened Pharaoh. So he did something awful. He gave out an order that every baby boy born in a Hebrew home should be snatched away and thrown into the river Nile. In this cruel way he hoped to stop the growth of these people. The mothers and fathers wept bitterly and tried to hide their children from Pharaoh's soldiers.

About this time, a Hebrew woman named Jochebed gave birth to a beautiful little boy. For three months she kept him hidden from Pharaoh's soldiers. But every passing footstep filled her with terror. She knew that if the soldiers heard his cries, they would take him away. "Oh, God," she prayed, "please save my precious baby."

Now, Jochebed also had a young daughter named Miriam. She was a brave and clever girl, and she loved her baby brother more than anything in the world. Together Jochebed and Miriam came up with a secret plan. They crept down to the river, gathered some reeds, and wove them into a basket. Then they covered it with mud and tar, so water could not get in. When the basket was finished, they kissed the baby, put him inside, and set it in the river. It floated safely at the stream's edge, hidden among the tall reeds, just like a little ark.

"I need you to stay here for a while," Jochebed told her daughter. "Watch the baby and see what happens."

So Miriam hid in a clump of bushes and kept guard. A gentle wind rippled along the shore, making the reeds whisper and sigh. Birds flitted by. Farther upstream, a great crocodile snorted, but he did not come near. The little basket rocked peacefully on the water. Miriam watched faithfully and knew, in her heart, that God was watching over her baby brother.

After a while, she heard voices and footsteps. She peeked out of her hiding place and drew in a sharp breath. Pharaoh's daughter was coming down to the river with her maidservants to bathe. The beautiful princess walked along the bank while her maidens followed, laughing and talking.

Suddenly the Egyptian princess spotted something floating among the reeds. "Quick, bring that basket to me," she called to one of her maidens. "I want to see if there is anything in it."

Miriam's heart beat faster. One of the maidservants waded into the stream and pulled the basket ashore.

The princess leaned over the basket and heard a baby's cry. Two little arms stretched toward her. She looked into the tiny face, and she was filled with pity and love for the beautiful boy.

"Why, this is a Hebrew baby!" the princess exclaimed. "He is hungry, poor thing." She smiled and wiped the tears from his little cheeks.

Miriam crouched in the bushes, thinking hard. The princess looked like a kind woman. Surely she would not let the baby die. So Miriam summoned all her courage and stepped out of her hiding place.

"Shall I go find one of the Hebrew women to nurse the child for you, and take care of it?" she asked the daughter of Pharaoh in a steady, clear voice.

"Yes," said the princess. "Go find a nurse for me."

Miriam's heart filled with joy. She ran home and told her mother everything that had happened. They hugged and kissed, and then hurried back to the princess.

"Take this child and nurse it for me," said the princess. "I will pay you to do so."

Jochebed took the baby into her arms and held him close. She felt the tiny heart beating through the blanket, and she could hardly keep back the tears. No one could harm her boy now, for he was protected by the princess of Egypt, the daughter of Pharaoh himself.

From that time on, the Egyptian soldiers did not dare come to Jochebed's home. Loved and tended by his own mother, the baby grew healthy and strong. His sister, Miriam, was always there too. She played with him, sang to him, and helped him learn how to walk and talk and do all the other things babies must learn.

When the boy grew older, he went to live in the royal palace. The princess treated him as if he were her own son, and she called him Moses.

Although Moses grew up among the Egyptians, he always loved his own people. They were only poor slaves, but he loved them because they served the Lord. Many years later, when he had grown up to be a man, Moses became a great leader of the Hebrew people. He led them out of Egypt, back to their own land, with his brave and wise sister, Miriam, at his side.

He Will Hear

☙ JANE TAYLOR

God hears us better when we make the effort to speak to him!

God is so good that he will hear
Whenever children humbly pray.
He always lends a gracious ear
To what the youngest child may say.

His own most holy Book declares
He loves good little children still,
And that he listens to their prayers
Just as a tender father will.

The Seed

As an old hymn puts it: We plow the fields and scatter the good seed on the land, but it is fed and watered by God's almighty hand.
All good gifts around us are sent from heaven above.

One warm autumn day a little girl dropped a seed into a hole in the ground, covered it up, and waited for her flower to grow.

Before long the winter snows arrived and left a thick white blanket all over the ground. And the poor seed could not grow at all.

After waiting patiently for weeks and months, the little girl peeked outside her door and said, "Now, seed, hurry and grow, grow, grow, until you have a tall stem covered with green leaves and big yellow blossoms."

But the seed answered, "I am still icy and cold. You must ask someone else."

"Who?" asked the little girl.

"The hard ground whose bed I lie in," said the seed.

"I will!" cried the little girl. "Ground, ground, won't you grow soft so my little seed can be warm and grow into a flower?"

But the ground answered, "You must ask someone else."

"Who?" asked the little girl.

"The snow who covers me," said the ground.

"I will!" cried the little girl. "Snow, snow, won't you melt away so the ground can grow soft, and my little seed can be warm, and grow into a flower?"

But the snow answered, "You must ask someone else."

"Who?" asked the little girl.

"The sun that melts me," said the snow.

"I will!" cried the little girl. "Sun, sun, won't you come out so the snow will melt, and the ground can grow soft, and my little seed can be warm, and grow into a flower?"

But the sun answered, "You must ask someone else."

"Who?" asked the little girl.

"The clouds that cover me," said the sun.

"I will!" cried the little girl. "Clouds, clouds, won't you go away so the sun can come out, and the snow can melt, and the ground can grow soft, and my little seed can be warm, and grow into a flower?"

But the clouds answered, "You must ask someone else."

"Who?" asked the little girl.

"The wind that blows us," said the clouds.

"I will!" cried the little girl. "Wind, wind, won't you blow so the clouds will go away, and the sun can come out, and the snow can melt, and the ground can grow soft, and my little seed can be warm, and grow into a flower?"

But the wind whispered in her ear, "You must ask someone else."

"Who?" asked the little girl.

"God, who makes all things grow," said the wind.

"I will!" cried the little girl. "I should have thought of that."

So she got down on her knees, and folded her hands, and prayed.

"God," she prayed, "won't you tell the wind to blow so the clouds will go away, and the sun can come out, and the snow can melt, and the ground can grow soft, and my little seed can be warm, and grow into a flower?"

And God smiled down on the little girl.

She looked out her door again. A warm breeze played in the air. The clouds were gone, the sun was shining, the snow was melting, and the ground was turning soft and green.

And before long her flower came up.

The Story of Hanukkah

The Jewish festival of Hanukkah celebrates the rededication of the temple in ancient Jerusalem after a triumph over the mighty Syrians. This is a story of tremendous bravery and faith in the struggle for religious freedom.

Long ago, the land of Israel was conquered by the Syrians and ruled by a king named Antiochus. This king was a wicked man. Always hungry for power and fame, he demanded that the Jews of Israel prove their loyalty to him by giving up their faith in God.

"From now on, you cannot worship your God," Antiochus told the Jews. "Instead, you must bow down to my god—the great Zeus."

Most of the Jews would not give up their faith, however, and went on worshipping God. When Antiochus heard how they disobeyed his command, he marched on Jerusalem with his army and looted the city. He entered the great temple, the holiest of places, and put up a statue of Zeus. Then he issued harsh orders. "If anyone does not worship as I tell them, they will be put to death," he announced.

The Jews knew that now they had no choice but to fight back. A few brave families went to live in caves in the hills. There they learned to fight with whatever weapons they could find or make—bows and arrows, slingshots, knives, even stones. More and more of their countrymen joined them, until they had a small army.

When Antiochus heard about these rebels, he sent an army to crush them. The mighty Syrians marched toward the hills: thousands of soldiers on horseback, thousands more on foot, and even huge elephants dressed for war. How could the Jews, with their small numbers and crude weapons, hope to defeat such a force?

Then a miracle of sorts happened. Again and again, the Jews turned back the armies of Antiochus. After three long years of war, the Syrians gave up and went home. The Jews won because they fought hard for freedom and for their right to worship God.

After their triumph, the first thing they did was to go to Jerusalem. What they saw made them heartsick. The gates

of the temple were burned. The walls were covered with filth and the floors littered with garbage. Wild animals roamed inside, and weeds grew all about the place.

At once they went to work. They built a new altar. They polished the temple floors, scrubbed the walls, and repaired the doors. At last everything was ready to offer thanks to God.

In the temple courtyard stood the menorah, a lamp meant to burn at all times. When the priests went to light it, they discovered they had only enough holy oil to last one day.

"There is no point in lighting it yet," cried one.

"We must have faith," said the high priest. He poured the oil into the lamp and lit it.

And then another miracle happened. The oil burned all day and all night. It burned the next day. And the next, and the next. The lamp burned for eight days, even though there was only enough oil for one. The people of Israel rejoiced, for they knew God was with them.

Every year, during the festival of Hanukkah, people of the Jewish faith celebrate by lighting menorahs in their homes. For eight nights, the light reminds the whole world that God is with us even during the darkest times. It reminds us all of those heroes of long ago who defeated a mighty empire. With courage and faith, they fought and won the freedom to worship God.

Why the Chimes Rang

RAYMOND ALDEN

Acts of kindness do not go unnoticed above,
even if they go unseen by the crowd below.

There was once in a faraway country a wonderful church with a gray stone tower, which had ivy growing up its sides as far up as the eye could see. In the tower hung the church's Christmas bells. They had hung there ever since the church had been built hundreds of years ago, and they were the most beautiful bells in the world.

For a long time, every Christmas Eve, all the people of the city would bring their offerings to the church to celebrate the birth of the Christ child. When the greatest and best offering was laid on the altar, the voices of the Christmas chimes would come sounding through the music of the choir. Some said the wind rang them, and others said they were so high up that the angels could set them swinging.

But the fact was that no one had heard the chimes for years and years. There was an old man living not far from the church, who said that his mother had spoken of hearing them when she was a little girl. But now it was said that the people were growing less careful of their gifts for the Christ child, and that none of the offerings they brought was great enough to deserve the music of the chimes.

People still crowded to the altar every Christmas Eve,

each one trying to bring some better gift than any other, although no one really ever gave anything that he wanted for himself. The church would be crowded with those who thought that perhaps the wonderful bells might be heard again. But although the service was splendid, and the offerings plenty, only the roar of the wind could be heard far up in the stone tower.

Now, a number of miles from the city, in a little country village, lived a boy named Pedro and his little brother. One year they decided to go see the beautiful celebration.

The day before Christmas was bitterly cold, with a few lonely snowflakes flying through the air, but the two boys started on their way to the Christmas celebration. Before nightfall they had trudged so far that they saw the lights of the city just ahead of them.

They were about to enter the city when they saw something dark on the snow near the path and stepped aside to look. It was a poor woman who had fallen. She was too sick and cold to get in where she might have found shelter.

Pedro knelt beside her and tugged at her arm. He tried rubbing some snow on her face, but she did not stir. He looked at her silently for a moment and then stood up again.

"It's no use, little brother," he said. "You will have to go on to the church alone."

"Alone?" cried the little brother. "And you will not see the Christmas festival?"

"No," said Pedro, and he could not help a little choking sound of disappointment in his throat. "See this poor woman. She will freeze to death if nobody cares for her. If you get a chance to slip up to the altar without getting in anyone's way, take this little silver piece of mine and lay it down for my offering, when no one is looking."

So he hurried his little brother off to the city, and blinked hard to keep back the tears as he heard the crunching footsteps sounding farther and farther away in the twilight. It was pretty hard to lose the splendor and music of the Christmas celebration and spend the time instead in that lonely place in the snow.

The great church was truly a wonderful sight that night. Everyone said that it had never looked so bright and beautiful. When the organ played and the people sang, the walls shook with the sound, and little Pedro, away outside the city, felt the earth tremble around him.

After the service, the people took their gifts to the altar. Some brought wonderful jewels, some baskets of gold so heavy that they could scarcely carry them down the aisle. A great writer laid down a book that he had been making for years and years. And last of all walked the king of the country, hoping with all the rest to win for himself the chime of the Christmas bells.

There was a murmur through the church as the people saw the king take from his head the royal crown, all set with diamonds and other precious stones, and lay it gleaming on the altar as his gift to honor the Christ child. "Surely," they said, "we shall hear the bells now."

But only the cold wind was heard in the tower, and the people shook their heads. Some of them said that they never really believed the story about the chimes, and doubted if they ever rang at all.

The celebration came to a close. The gifts were on the altar, and the choir began the closing hymn. Suddenly the organist stopped playing, and everyone looked at the old minister, who was standing in his place and holding up his hand for silence. Not a sound could be heard from anyone in the church, but as the people strained their ears to listen, there came softly but distinctly, swinging through the air, the sound of the bells in the tower!

So far away and yet so clear seemed the music, so much sweeter were the notes than anything else that had been heard before, rising and falling away up there in the sky, that the people in the church sat for a moment very still. Then they all stood up together and stared at the altar, to see what great gift had awakened the long-silent bells.

But all that the nearest of them saw was the childish figure of Pedro's brother, who had crept softly down the aisle when no one was looking, and had laid Pedro's little piece of silver on the altar.

My Gift

CHRISTINA ROSSETTI

Silver and gold have I none; but such as I have give I thee. —ACTS 3:6

What can I give Him
Poor as I am?
If I were a shepherd
I would give him a lamb.
If I were a wise man,
I would do my part.
Yet what can I give Him?
Give my heart.

Loving Jesus

~ CHARLES WESLEY

Faith helps us learn how to be good while we grow.

Loving Jesus, meek and mild,
Look upon a little child!
Make me gentle as Thou art,
Come and live within my heart.
Take my childish hand in Thine,
Guide these little feet of mine.
So shall all my happy days
Sing their pleasant song of praise,
And the world shall always see
Christ, the Holy Child, in me.

The Lord's Prayer

As Christ has taught us, we are bold to say —

Our Father, who art in heaven,
    hallowed be thy Name;
    thy kingdom come,
    thy will be done,
    on earth as it is in heaven.
Give us this day our daily bread.
And forgive us our trespasses,
    as we forgive those
    who trespass against us.
And lead us not into temptation,
    but deliver us from evil.
For thine is the kingdom,
    and the power, and the glory,
    for ever and ever.
        Amen.

Bedtime Prayers

*At bedtime, prayer is the key that closes our day
and reminds us of God's care.*

Now I lay me down to sleep,
I pray the Lord my soul to keep.
If I should die before I wake,
I pray the Lord my soul to take.
                    Amen.

Heavenly Father, hear my prayer,
Take thy child into thy care.
Let thy angels pure and bright
Watch around me through the night.
                    Amen.

Blessed Lord, we thank you
For your care today.
Make us good and gentle,
Take our sins away.
Bless the friends who love us,
From all evil keep.
May your holy angels
Guard us while we sleep.
                    Amen.

I hear no voice, I feel no touch,
I see no glory bright,
But yet I know that God is near
In darkness as in light.
He watches ever by my side,
And hears my whispered prayer.
The Father for his little child
Both day and night does care.
                    Amen.

Saint Augustine's
Walk by the Sea

*This legend reminds us that there are many things we can learn and know,
but there are also things we must leave to God.*

Saint Augustine was one of the wisest and most learned of men. He loved to study and read, and he loved to think about God. He could spend hours and hours pondering God's creation and his mysterious ways.

One day Saint Augustine was taking a stroll by the sea. It was a bright day with hardly a cloud in the sky. The golden sun sparkled on the water. Seagulls drifted on the breeze, calling to one another. The waves made a cheerful sound as they lapped the shore.

But Saint Augustine did not really notice the blue sky, or the sparkling sun, or the cry of the seagulls. He was deep in thought. He longed to know the answers to all sorts of questions. Why does God let bad things happen sometimes? Why can't we see him? Where is heaven? They were all difficult questions, but Saint Augustine hoped that if he thought about them long and hard enough, surely he could understand God's great plan.

He thought and he thought, but he could not discover the answers. The more he thought, the less he seemed to know. After a while, he began to feel sad and even a little bit angry that he could not understand so many things that God does.

Suddenly he came upon a little boy who had dug a hole in the sand. The boy filled a bucket at the edge of the water, ran and poured it into the hole, and then went back to the sea for more water.

Now, if you have ever been to the beach, you know that the sand does not hold water. If you dig a hole and pour water into it, the water just runs through the sand at the bottom of the hole. You can pour and pour, but the hole will never fill up.

The little boy kept emptying bucket after bucket into the hole he had dug. Again and again he poured out the water, and then hurried back to the sea to refill his pail.

Saint Augustine watched from a distance for a while, and then walked over to the child. "What are you doing, my boy?" he asked.

The child did not show any surprise at the question. "I'm going to pour all the water of the ocean into this hole," he answered.

"But that is not possible!" Saint Augustine said with a smile. "You cannot do it."

The little boy looked up at him.

"That is right," he said quietly. "Just as you cannot understand all the mysteries of God."

At once Saint Augustine caught the truth of these simple words. Then he saw that it was not a child who spoke to him, but a beautiful angel.

All the sadness left his heart, and it filled with joy. He bowed his head, closed his eyes, and gave thanks, because he realized that many of God's acts must remain a mystery to us. We cannot understand them, no matter how hard we try. It is impossible for us to know all of God's plan, just as it is impossible to pour the great ocean into a hole in the sand. So we must have faith and believe.

When Saint Augustine raised his head and opened his eyes, he was alone with the sea and sand and sky.